C000178136

SHORT CIRC
Il
SOUTH DERBYSHIRE

by
JOHN N. MERRILL

Maps and photographs by John N. Merrill.

a J.N.M. Publication

1990

a J.N.M. PUBLICATION,

J.N.M. PUBLICATIONS,
WINSTER,
MATLOCK,
DERBYSHIRE.
DE4 2DQ
℗ Winster (062988) 454
Fax: Winster (062988) 416

Conceived, edited, typeset, designed, paged, marketed and distributed by John N. Merrill.

© Text and Routes - John N. Merrill 1990.

© Maps and photographs - John N. Merrill 1990.

First Published - September 1987 as "Short Circular Walks around Derby" - ISBN 0 907496 49 0
This edition - June 1990.

ISBN 0 907496 87 3

Meticulous research has been undertaken to ensure that this publication is highly accurate at the time of going to press. The publishers, however, cannot be held responsible for alterations, errors or omissions, but they would welcome notification of such for future editions.

Typeset in - Bookman - bold, italic and plain 9pt and 18pt.

Printed by - Elgar Printing Ltd., Hereford.

Cover Sketch - Anchor Church, Nr. Ingleby by John Creber © J.N.M. PUBLICATIONS 1990.

An all British product.

ABOUT
JOHN N. MERRILL

John combines the characteristics and strength of a mountain climber with the stamina and athletic capabilities of a marathon runner. In this respect he is unique and has to his credit a whole string of remarkable long walks. He is without question the world's leading marathon walker.

Over the last fifteen years he has walked more than 100,000 miles and successfully completed ten walks of a least 1,000 miles or more. His six major walks in Great Britain are -

Hebridean Journey....... 1,003 miles.
Northern Isles Journey......913 miles.
Irish Island Journey ....1,578 miles.
Parkland Journey.......2,043 miles.
Land's End to John o' Groats.....1,608 miles.

and in 1978 he became the first person (permanent Guinness Book of Records entry) to walk the entire coastline of Britain - 6,824 miles in ten months.

In Europe he has walked across Austria - 712 miles - hiked the Tour of Mont Blanc, completed High Level Routes in the Dolomites and Italian Alps, and the GR20 route across Corsica in training! In 1982 he walked across Europe - 2,806 miles in 107 days - crossing seven countries, the Swiss and French Alps and the complete Pyrennean chain - the hardest and longest mountain walk in Europe, with more than 600,000 feet of ascent!

In America he used The Appalachian Trail - 2,200 miles - as a training walk, He has walked from Mexico to Canada via the Pacific Crest Trail in record time - 118 days for 2,700 miles. He has walked most of the Continental Divide Trail and much of New Mexico; his second home. In Canada he has walked the Rideau Trail - Kingston to Ottowa - 220 miles and The Bruce Trail - Tobermory to Niagara Falls - 460 miles.

In 1984 John set off from Virginia Beach on the Atlantic coast, and walked 4,226 miles without a rest day, across the width of America to Santa Cruz and San Francisco on the Pacific coast. His walk is unquestionably his greatest achievement, being, in modern history, the longest, hardest crossing of the U.S.A. in the shortest time - under six months (178 days). The direct distance is 2,800 miles.

Between major walks John is out training in his own area - The Peak District National Park. He has walked all of our National Trails many times - The Cleveland Way thirteen times and The Pennine Way four times in a year! He has been trekking in the Himalayas five times. He created more than a dozen challenge walks which have been used to raise more than £250,000 for charity. From his own walks he has raised over £100,000. He is author of more than one hundred walking guides; most of which he publishes himself, His book sales are in excess of 2 1/2 million, He has created many long distance walks including The Limey Way , The Peakland Way, Dark Peak Challenge walk, and Rivers' Way. He lectures extensively in Britain and America.

CONTENTS

INTRODUCTION

To many, Derbyshire walking means the Peak District. but the National Park occupies only a third of the county. As a result the remainder of the county is neglected by the majority, which is good in some ways, as it means one has the countryside to enjoy alone most of the time. But, it also means the rights of way are not used or maintained as they ought to be. This has resulted in some areas being quite hard to walk in as rights of way become overgrown. Whilst the Peak District may have its scenic splendour, the countryside to the south is particularly attractive and crammed with places of historical interest.

This is what makes walking in South Derbyshire so worthwhile, for you not only get some good exercise but discover and learn about highly interesting surroundings. The walks I have devised endeavour to illustrate the variety of walking to be found. Some are on good paths exploring distant views; others take you into unfrequented locations with stunning buildings and historical churches; whilst others enable you to appreciate the craft of man to create and build in such incomparable settings. The walks take you into woodland, open fields, lanes, beside canals and to lofty vantage points.

Being more rural country you will find some of the paths overgrown in summer, but don't be put off, it is all part of walking in the countryside. I have attempted to give as many walking instructions as possible to enable you to find your way with my map, but it is always wise to carry the appropriate 1:25,000 Ordnance Survey map to enable you to appreciate more of the area.

I have spent almost four months walking in the area checking and seeking out the paths detailed in this book and unbelievably met no other walkers! So, here is a slice of Derbyshire for you to explore and get to know on foot. The Dale and Morley area remain one of favourite places, but the Doveridge, Belper, and Ingleby walks arc some of the most enjoyable walks I have ever done in Derbyshire. I hope the walks in this book give you added pleasure in walking the area and I hope you, like me, discover the many secrets and remarkable places it has to offer. Quite simply, have a good walk and may the sun shine all day

HAPPY WALKING!

John N. Merrill

Winster, Derbyshire. 1990.

TRENT & MERSEY CANAL, NR. WILLINGTON.

MORLEY CROSS.

ABOUT THE WALKS

Whilst every care is taken detailing and describing the walks in this book, it should be borne in mind that the countryside changes by the seasons and the work of man. I have described the walks to the best of my ability, detailing what I have found on the walk in the way of stiles and signs. Obviously with the passage of time stiles become broken or replaced by a ladder stile or even a small gate. Signs too have a habit of being broken or pushed over. All the routes follow rights of way and only on rare occasions will you have to overcome obstacles in its path, such as a barbed wire fence or electric fence.

The seasons bring occasional problems whilst out walking which should also be borne in mind. In the height of summer paths become overgrown and you will have to fight your way through in a few places. In low lying areas the fields are often full of crops, and although the pathline goes straight across it may be more practical to walk round the field edge to get to the next stile or gate. In summer the ground is generally dry but in autumn and winter, especially because of our climate, the surface can be decidedly wet and slippery; sometimes even gluttonous mud!

These comments are part of countryside walking which help to make your walk more interesting or briefly frustrating. Standing in a farmyard up to your ankles in mud might not be funny at the time but upon reflection was one of the highlights of the walk!

The mileage for each walk is based on three calculations -

1. pedometer reading.
2. the route map measured on the map.
3. the time I took for the walk.

I believe the figure stated for each walk to be very accurate but we all walk differently and not always in a straight line! The time allowed for each walk is on the generous side and does not include pub stops etc. The figure is based on the fact that on average a person walks 2 1/2 miles an hours but less in hilly terrain.

DALE AND LOCKO PARK - 4 1/2 MILES

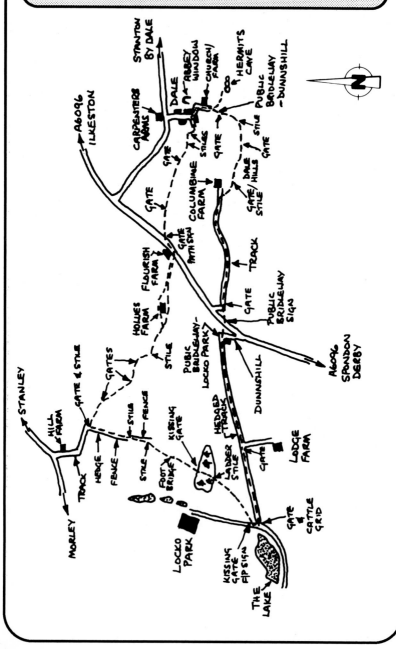

DALE AND LOCKO PARK —4 1/2 MILES - allow 2 1/2 hours

•▪◦•▪◦ •▪◦•▪◦ —*Dale—Dale Hills—Dunnshill—Locko Park (the Lake)— Hill Farm —Hollies Farm—The Flourish—Dale.*

 O.S. 1:25,000 Pathfinder series Sheet No SK 43/53—Nottingham (South West).

—*no official one*

ABOUT THE WALK—Dale is a fascinating area with the remains of an Abbey, hermits cave and minute church. The walk takes you close to these, allowing easy access to explore further before walking beneath the remarkably attractive Dale Hills. Crossing the A6096 road you enter Locko Park and get extensive views of the house and lake. You return across the fields to The Flourish and gradually descend back into Dale.

WALKING INSTRUCTIONS—Starting in Dale just down from the Carpenters Arms walk through the village past Abbey House and solitary ruined window in the field beyond. Continue towards the church now on a bridlepath as you follow the track to the farm on the righthand side of the church. Here, as bridlepath signed— Dunnshill— go through the gate and follow the defined path. The track to your left leads to the Hermit's Cave. The path bears left to a stile before entering woodland and keeping to its righthand side. It is particularly attractive here in Spring when the ground is covered with bluebells. Pass through a gate into more open country with the Dale Hills above on your left. Keep on the track with the field boundary on your right as you round Columbine Farm to your right. On the other side join the farm track as you ascend to the road (A6096) and Dunnshill. Where the track turns sharp right to the road, keep ahead on the track through the bushes to gain the road and bridlepath sign.

Cross the road and ascend to the track with bridlepath sign—Locko Park on the right of Dunns Hill Cottage. Keep on the hedged track for the next 1/2 mile into Locko Park. The track is now tarmaced, and almost 1/2 mile later approach The Lake. Here turn right and right again through the kissing gate beside the path sign and ascend the well defined path towards the wood with views of the house to your left. A metal ladder stile leads you into the wood, and at the other side a metal kissing gate enters into the fields. Keep the fence on your right and soon cross a footbridge with a wood on your right. Continue ahead, ascending gradually to a stile by the other end of the wood. Keep the fence on your right to the next stile, after which the fence is now on your left. At the end of the second field gain the track from Hill Farm at a gate and stile, and turn right.

The hedge is on your right to the next two gates as you begin reaching a fenced/hedged track. Continue along it to a gate then stile ahead. The track now turns left to Hollies Farm. This is a right of way and can be followed around the lefthand side of the farm and on the farm road to the A6096 road. Another right of way is just over the stile turn left keeping the field boundary on your left all the way

to the gate close to the A6096 road. On your left is the former Flourish Inn. Cross the road to your left and a few yards later reach the gate and path sign. At first you follow a grass track across the field to a gate. You are now descending gently with the field boundary on your left as you pass through a gap then gate in the next field. Through this cross the field to its pointed end and reach a stile. You are now on a hedged track and almost back into Dale. After a few yards turn right through a stile—you can keep straight ahead back into Dale. Descend the path to your left to the road and thatched shed on your right. Walk along the road back into Dale where you began. The Carpenters Arms is up the road to your left.

LOCKO PARK—The chapel dates from 1669 but the main building dates from the mid 18th century when the Lowe family took up residence in 1745. Since then the building has been given an Italian style last century. A major riding event takes place here each year.

DALE—Little remains of the Abbey that stood here following its destruction m Henry V111's reign apart from some walls incorporated in some of todays buildings. The prominent feature is the 40 foot high window archway standing alone in a nearby field. The stained glass windows were saved and are now in Morley Church, four miles away and are an exceptionally colourful display. In Dale is a hermit's cave and the church and farm are one building; at one time the farm was an inn! At The Flourish, this was also a former inn.

MORLEY— The church dedicated to St. Matthew is one of the most interesting in Derbyshire with considerable Norman workmanship and mediaeval stained glass windows from Dale Abbey. The tower and spire are early 15th century.

LOCKO PARK.

ABBEY HOUSE, DALE.

11

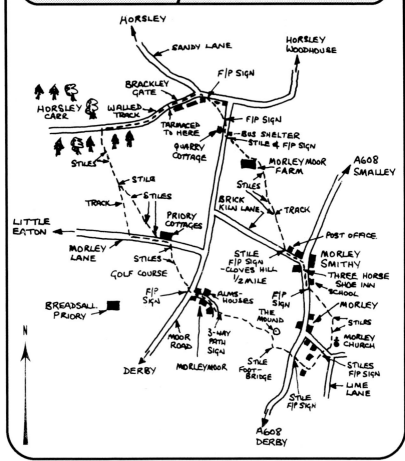

MORLEY & HORSLEY CARR - 4 1/2 MILES

HORSLEY

SANDY LANE

HORSLEY WOODHOUSE

F/P SIGN

BRACKLEY GATE

HORSLEY CARR

WALLED TRACK

TARMACED TO HERE

F/P SIGN

BUS SHELTER STILE & F/P SIGN

QUARRY COTTAGE

MORLEYMOOR FARM

A608 SMALLEY

STILES

STILE

STILES

STILES

BRICK KILN LANE

TRACK

TRACK

POST OFFICE

LITTLE EATON

PRIORY COTTAGES

MORLEY LANE

STILES

GOLF COURSE

STILE F/P SIGN -CLOVES HILL 1/2 MILE

MORLEY SMITHY

THREE HORSE SHOE INN

SCHOOL

BREADSALL PRIORY

N

F/P SIGN

ALMS-HOUSES

F/P SIGN

MORLEY

STILES

THE MOUND

MORLEY CHURCH

MOOR ROAD

3-WAY PATH SIGN

STILE FOOT-BRIDGE

STILES F/P SIGN

LIME LANE

DERBY

MORLEYMOOR

STILE F/P SIGN

A608 DERBY

THREE HORSE SHOE INN, MORLEY SMITHY.

MORLEY & HORSLEY CARR
—4 1/2 MILES - allow 2 hours

 —*Morley church—Morleymoor—Breadsall Moor— Horsley Carr— Brackely Gate—Morleymoor Farm—Morley Smithy— Morley.*

 —*1:25,000 O.S. Pathfinder Series Sheet No SK 24/34—Belper.*

—*no official one.*

ABOUT THE WALK—Morley church contains some of the finest stained glass windows in the country. A visit here is a must, and the exceptional high quality is maintained as you walk round this route; surprisingly near to Derby. The paths are little used but all the stiles are there and you should find no difficulty, apart from long grass in summer. You pass interesting buildings, delightful woodland and an inn towards the end! For me, and I hope for you, this walk is one of the most enjoyable in the area.

WALKING INSTRUCTIONS—I have started the walk from Morley Church, but, as with the rest of the walk, there is very little parking space close by. However, opposite the church drive entrance is a stile and a footpath sign. Pass through the stile and another immediately after, and walk up the field with the field boundary on your right. At the top go through a gate and slightly right to a stile. Through this turn right to another a few yards away. Although it seems you are doubling back on yourself, cross the field corner to another stile. Over this and the path becomes more obvious as you cross the field to a stile, path sign and descend to the A608. Cross to your right to a track and path sign. Follow the track for a 100 yards to a stile on your right. Turn right through this and across a footbridge and keep to the field edge on your left to approach a prominent tree- covered mound ahead. Here gain a hedged track which you follow to your left. At its end emerge into a large field. The true right of way goes across it but it is perhaps simpler to keep on the track around its lefthand edge. At the far side turn right on a path to a prominent triple path sign. Turn left through the stile into Morley Almshouses Lane. Bear right along it past the Almshouses on your right to Moor Road.

Go straight across by the telephone kiosk and follow the signed path—a track at first past the allotments and then into a field. Now you follow a path which reaches a stile in the far righthand corner of the field. Through this you keep the field edge on your left as you head for Morley Lane and Priory Cottages just ahead. On your left is Breadsall Priory golf course. At the lane turn left past the cottages. On the far left of them is a stile and right of way diagonally across three fields. It is well stiled. Instead of using this path you can continue down the lane for 150 yards to a pathsign on your right and turn right along a track. The other path comes into this. Keep on this track for 1/2 mile to a stile on the edge of Moor Plantation. Continue ahead on the track through the trees and descend to a walled track. Here turn right, still in woodland, and follow it for a little over 1/2 mile into Brackely Gate. At the road junction turn right and right again almost immediately at the path sign close to Melville House. The path is well defined and fenced as you pass between the houses and in 1/4 mile reach Quarry Road.

Turn right, and after about 100 yards just past a bus shelter on your left is the stile and path sign. The path is ill-defined but go diagonally across the field to your right, aiming for the gate on the left of Morleymoor Farm. Walk round to your right past the buildings to a stile. Cross the farm drive to another stile and descend the field towards the lefthand corner where there is a stile. Over this turn left and keep the field boundary on your left all the way to Morley Smithy, a little over 1/4 mile away, emerging onto the road via a stile beside the path sign—Cloves Hill 1/2 mile. Turn left along Brick Kiln Lane to the A608 road and the Three Horse Shoes Inn on your right. Turn right along the road past Morley School on your left to a path sign just afterwards on your left. The pathline goes diagonally across the large field to a stile. As you cross the spire of Morley Church acts as a useful guide, although at this stage you should aim well to the left of it. Once at the stile you now head for it across the field, then beside the church wall to a stile and into the churchyard. A little to your left is the church and to your right is Morley Cross and the church drive where you began.

EAST MILL, BELPER.

BELPER & CHEVIN - 6 MILES

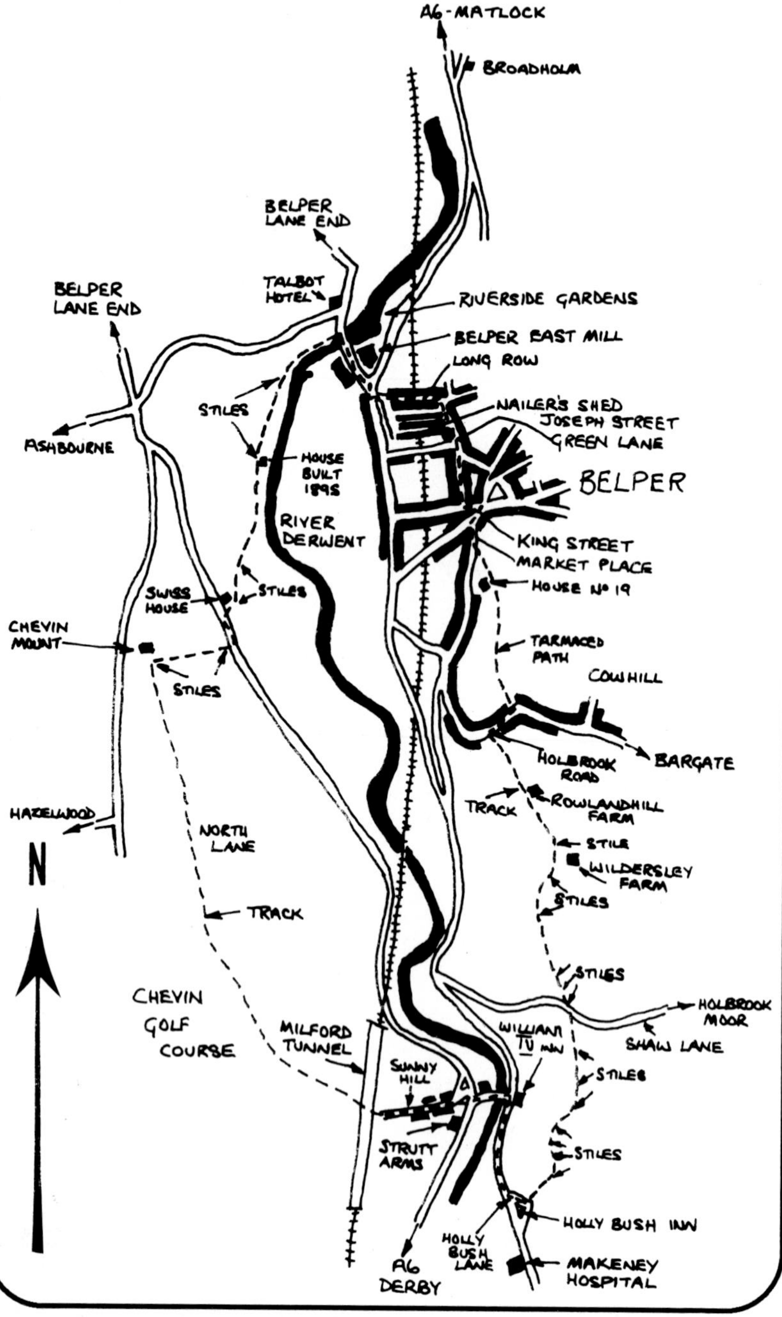

A6 - MATLOCK

BROADHOLM

BELPER LANE END

TALBOT HOTEL

BELPER LANE END

RIVERSIDE GARDENS

BELPER EAST MILL
LONG ROW

STILES

ASHBOURNE

NAILER'S SHED
JOSEPH STREET
GREEN LANE

HOUSE BUILT 1895

BELPER

RIVER DERWENT

KING STREET
MARKET PLACE

SWISS HOUSE

STILES

HOUSE No 19

CHEVIN MOUNT

TARMACED PATH

COW HILL

STILES

BARGATE

HOLBROOK ROAD

ROWLANDHILL FARM

HAZELWOOD

TRACK

NORTH LANE

STILE

WILDERSLEY FARM

STILES

N

TRACK

STILES

HOLBROOK MOOR

CHEVIN GOLF COURSE

MILFORD TUNNEL

WILLIAM IV INN

SHAW LANE

SUNNY HILL

STILES

STRUTT ARMS

STILES

HOLLY BUSH INN

HOLLY BUSH LANE

MAKENEY HOSPITAL

A6 DERBY

16

BELPER AND CHEVIN—6 miles
- allow 3 hours

  —*Belper (East Mill)—River Derwent—Chevin (North Lane)—Milford—Makeney—Wildersley Farm—Cowhill—Belper (East Mill).*

—*O.S. 1:25,000 Pathfinder Series Sheet No SK24/34—Belper*

—*No official one.*

ABOUT THE WALK—Belper's history is fascinating with its mills and nail industry. This walk takes you past many of its key features while ascending the Chevin ridge and providing impressive views to the north and south of the Derwent valley. Although close to a populated area I believe you will be surprised at the quality of the walking and there are several inns along the way!

WALKING INSTRUCTIONS—Starting from East Mill in Belper, walk past the mill and cross Belper Bridge over the River Derwent. Turn left immediately onto the fenced track above the river. Soon pass through a stile and continue on the path with a wall on your left. 1/4 mile later gain another stile and continue ahead; on your left is an attractive house built in 1895. The path now takes you back to the river on your left. Notice a stile on your right in the wall, but don't take this one. 75 yards later take the next stile on your right, and follow the defined ascending path to your left, en route passing a well on your left and two more stiles before gaining a wooden one on the immediate left of Swiss House. Walk down the drive to the minor road and turn left. Two fields later turn right at the double stile and ascend to the track on the left of Chevin Mount. Turn left and follow this track—North Lane—for the next 1 1/2 miles. Ignore all branches, and eventually after passing the Chevin Golf Course gain the tarmaced road as you descend steeply—Sunny Hill. At the bottom continue ahead down Chevin Alley to the A6 road in Milford. On your right is The Strutt Arms Hotel.

Turn left along the A6 past Milford Mill and over the Derwent. Turn right in front of William IV Inn onto the Makeney road. Pass the Garden Centre on your right and before Makeney Hospital turn left up Holly Bush Lane. At the top with the Holly Bush Inn on your right, turn left up the lane to a bridlepath sign and bridleway. Go through the stile on your left and walk around the field to a stile. Just after this one turn right through a stone stile and follow the defined path as you descend and ascend to Shaw Lane, almost 1/2 mile away. The path is well stiled. Cross the lane and as signed keep ahead on the path along the field edge. Pass through several stiles and gain a small wood. Here the path divides. Turn right through the stile and walk with the wood on your immediate left. Keep to the left of Wildersley Farm and gain a track which you follow past Rowlandhill Farm to Holbrook Road. Turn right up the road, and on the sharp righthand corner turn left onto a tarmaced path between the houses and open fields, then past houses on your left. Much of it is tarmaced as you descend to more houses, walking past No 19 to the road in Belper. Continue ahead ascending towards the Market Place. At the junction with King Street—Belper's main shopping area—turn left then right into Green Lane. Keep straight ahead on this road past the church on your right. Shortly afterwards on your left is Joseph Street and a few yards down here is the only Belper Nailers workshop. Continue on the road to its end and turn left into Long Row, a cobbled street with mill worker's cottages on either side. Descend this to the A6 road. To your right is East Mill where you began.

BELPER—For several centuries the town was a major producer of nails, but today only one of their workshops remains. In 1776 the cotton mill began production and grew to today's impressive East Mill, with adjacent weirs and water canals. Long Row is a particularly fine example of Industrial housing for the cotton workers.

MILFORD—The mill was founded by Jedediah Strutt, as the nearby inn retains his memory. Alas the mill has now closed.

NAILER'S SHOP, BELPER.

LONG ROW, BELPER.

RIVER DERWENT & EAST MILL, BELPER.

IDRIDGEHAY AND IRETON WOOD - 5 MILES

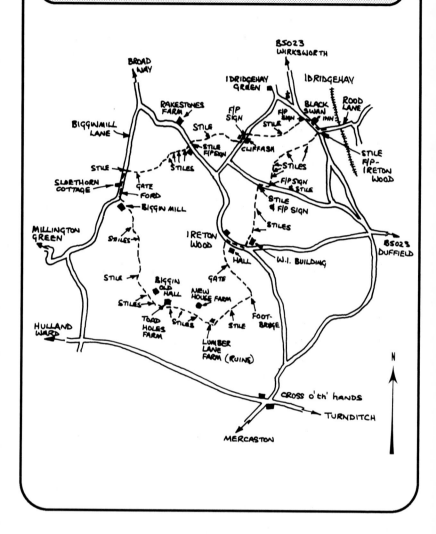

20

IDRIDGEHAY AND IRETON WOOD—5 miles - allow 2 1/2 hours

  —Idridgehay—Windley Lane—Ireton Wood—Lumber Lane Farm— Toad Holes Farm—Biggin Old Hall—Biggin Mill—Gorses—Cliffash— Idridgehay.

—O.S. 1:25,000 Pathfinder Series Sheet No SK 24/34—Belper

—No official one.

ABOUT THE WALK—The area is riddled with footpaths which are rarely used, despite its being a hilly and extremely attractive area. In the main the path signs and stiles are there, but in a few places they don't exist. Don't let this put you off, for the walk passes through an unspoilt corner of Derbyshire which will come as quite a surprise! The only inn is at the end of the walk. I have started the walk from the road junction just down from the Black Swan Inn in Idridgehay, at Rood Lane.

WALKING INSTRUCTIONS—Opposite the road junction, to the right, is the stile and footpath sign—Ireton Wood. Go through the stile and cross the field to your left to a gate. Through this bear right as you ascend the field to a stile on the edge of Carr Wood. Keep the wood on your left to the next stile. Bear left with the hedge on your right to the next stile and another beside a footpath sign and Windley Lane. T urn right and after 50 yards, at the second path sign, turn left through the stile. Keep the hedge on your left to the next stile; then keep it on your right past pine trees as you descend to another stile on your right. over this keep the hedge on your left as you descend to a stile by a stream . Over this pass the W . I . building on your left and gain the road at Ireton Wood. Turn right, and just after the entrance gates to Ireton Wood Hall turn left at the next gate with path sign a little to your right. Keep to the edge of the woodland of the Hall as you curve round to your left to gain a track and gate. You then walk across the middle of a large field to left of woodland and small lake. On your left is the wooden footbridge.

Over this bear right, keeping the woodland on your right as you ascend the field edge to a stile and gate at the top of the next field. Turn right onto the track to New House Farm, but where it turns right leave it for the wooden stile beside the rhododendron bush. The pathline is now westwards across the middle of two fields and is well stiled. After this the path keeps close to the hedge on your right and cross a small tree covered ditch to the next stile. over this and you pass Toad Holes Farm on your right. Cross the track to another stile and afterwards gain another stile a few yards later with Biggin Old Hall on your right. Another stile follows immediately and you -hen descend the held to a stream. Don't cross it instead turn right beside it passing a footbridgc on your Ieft. About 50 yards later gain a stile and cross the stream and ascend to your right to another stile and gate in the righthand corner of the field. Turn Ieft, and ahead can be seen the wooden stile with woodland on your right . Keep this on your right to the next stile. After this keep the Sherbourne Brook on your right as you walk past Biggin Mill on your left to Bigginmill Lane.

Turn right and over the footbridge, with the ford on your right. Ascend past Sloehorn Cottage, and at the end of the second field on your right turn right over the vvooden stile. Keep a lookout for this one. Keep the field boundary on your left as you descend to a fixed gate. Ascend this and continue ahead ascending with a small stream on your right; later this becomes a hedge before gaining a stone stile.

Continue ascending with the field boundary on your right. The next stile is missing, but just over the field end can be seen the next stile. Ascend and curve to your left to the next stile with a house on your right. Continue to the road, gained via a gate beside a path sign. Turn right and left almost immediately at the next stile and footpath sign. You are now heading easterly as you curve round to another stile and then cross three fields to the south of Çliffash, none of which have proper field boundaries. Gain the road via a gate and turn left to Cliffash Farm. A few yards later turn right at the footpath sign and descend past the farm on your right. Keep the field boundary on your left to a stile on your left. Over this keep the field boundary on your right as you descend to the B5023 road, gained by a gate beside a path sign. As you descend the spire of Idridgehay Church is to your left and the Black Swan Inn to your right. Turn right to Rood Lane where you began.

IDRIDGEHAY—The church dedicated to St. James dates from 1854.

BIGGIN OLD HALL.

BLACK SWAN INN, IDRIDGEHAY.

MUGGINGTON AND WESTON UNDERWOOD - 4 MILES

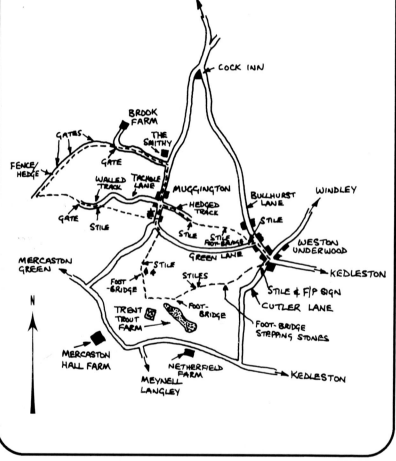

MUGGINGTON AND WESTON UNDERWOOD—4 MILES
- allow 1 1/2 hours

 — *Muggington — Trent Trout Farm — Weston Underwood — Muggington—Hungerhill Brook—Muggington.*

 —*1:25,000 O.S. Pathfinder Series—Sheet No SK 24/34— Belper.*

—*no official one.*

ABOUT THE WALK—a short figure of eight walk which can be two separate walks of approximately 2 miles each. The area is little walked but is a very attractive secluded locality with all the signs and stiles in place. The principal attraction, apart from the solitude, is the remarkably attractive Muggington Church whose beam ceilings are more than worth a cursory glance. There is no inn on the walk but the Cock Inn lies just to the north of both villages.

WALKING INSTRUCTIONS—Starting from Muggington Church, which as you walk through it at the end of the walk is best left till then to explore. Descend to the road junction just below the church and turn left into Green Lane. Almost immediately turn right through a gate gap and descend the field with the hedge and fence on your right to a stile and pine trees. Walk through these to another stile and footbridge over Mercaston Brook. Turn half left and ascend gently to the water channel and keep it on your right to the first bridge. Here turn left beside the fence with the trout ponds on your right to reach a footbridge. Ascend diagonally to your right across the field to a stile. Cross to another and descend to a stile, footbridge and stepping stones. Ascend the prominent ridge ahead with the farm on your right to eventually reach a stile and path sign close to Cutler Lane on the outskirts of Weston Underwood. Turn left along the lane to the cross roads and turn left along Bullhurst Lane. Take the first road on your left—Green Lane—soon afterwards and immediately turn right through the stile on your right and descend to a footbridge over Greenlane Brook. Ascend the field beyond with the field boundary on your right to gain a stile. Continue ahead into a hedged track which you follow back into Muggington. The church is to your left.

Turn right and ascend Church Lane past the houses to the first track on your left before the house, The Smithy. Descend this and after 1/4 mile cross Hungerhill Brook. Here the track swings right to Brook Farm. Leave it here via the gate on your left and ascend the track with the hedge on your right. The track eventually disappears but the next three fields are gained by gates, with the field boundary always on your right . In the fourth field, in its bottom righthand corner, you turn left and join a defined path which soon becomes a walled track—Tachole Lane—which you can follow back to Muggington, entering almost opposite to where you came in. However, just after entering the walled track, on your right is a stile and by going over this and turning left you can ascend towards the church, via the stiled fields, entering the churchyard of Muggington church. The other side is the road where you began.

MUGGINGTON CHURCH—dedicated to All Saints it dates from the 12th century and has many notable gargoyle carvings.

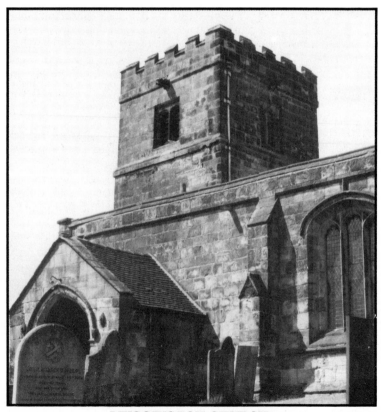

MUGGINGTON CHURCH.

VIEW TO TRENT TROUT FARMS, MUGGINGTON.

CHALYBEATE WELL, QUARNDON.

DUFFIELD
& BUNKER'S HILL - 6 MILES

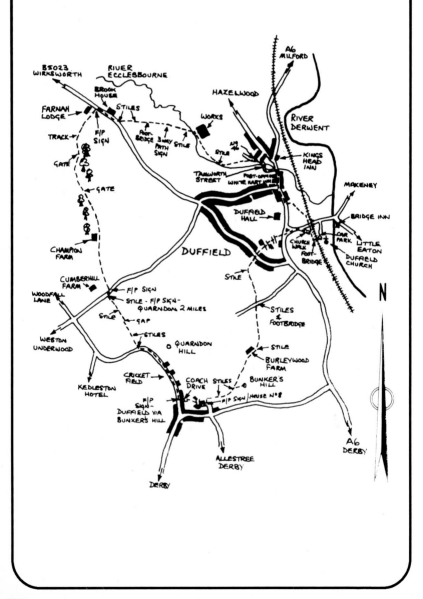

DUFFIELD AND BUNKER'S HILL—6 MILES
- allow 2 1/2 hours

 —Duffield Church—Duffield—Duffield Meadows— Farnah Lodge— Champion Farm—Cumberhill Farm—Quarndon— Bunker's Hill—Burleywood Farm—Duffield—Duffield church.

 —1:25,000 O.S. Pathfinder Series Sheet No SK 24/34—Belper.

—Eyes Meadows, close to Duffield Church.

ABOUT THE WALK—Duffield has numerous historical buildings which you see as you walk through. After crossing Duffield Meadows and River Ecclesbourne you begin the long but gentle ascent towards Quarndon with extensive views over the Derwent Valley. Skirting the northern edge of Quarndon you gain Bunker's Hill, whose viewpoint is one of the most extensive in the Derby area. You descend the fields and through part of Duffield back to its historic church. Apart from inns in Duffield, the route is dry! The Bridge Inn beside the River Derwent is not far from Duffield Church.

WALKING INSTRUCTIONS—From the car park walk towards the church entrance and turn right to ascend the foot-bridge over the railway. Turn right and almost immediately, where the road turns sharp left, keep ahead on a path which keeps close to the railway line on your right. Pass through stiles under the road bridge ahead, and the defined path soon angles left to a stile before the A6 road. On your left across the road is Duffield Hall, now the home of the Derbyshire Building Society. Turn right along the A6 in central Duffield past the Post Office and White Hart Inn. Just before the Kings Head Inn, turn left along Tamworth Street, passing The Park on your left. Follow the street round to the right and at the road junction left along Crown Street. After a few yards near house No 46 turn left along a tarmaced surface, past the Fire Station on your right and close to the River Ecclesbourne. At the bridge over it, keep ahead via the stile and follow the path across the field to a factory and path sign. Turn left through the premises to a stile and meadows. Another stile follows 30 yards later, and once over this aim for the metal triple footpath sign. Here continue diagonally across the field, as signed— Wirksworth Road

29

1/2 mile. The path is undefined but you should have no problem locating the footbridge over the stream. Bear right slightly in the next field to the stile and in the following field the path sign can be seen ahead on your left, beside a stile. on the other side is the Wirksworth Road—B5023.

Turn right along the road past Brook House on your right and shortly after turn left through the gate of Farnah Lodge, and walk along the track. You keep on this track for the next 1 1/2 miles as you walk beside woodland on your left as you begin to ascend the gated track. At the second gate woodland is now on your right . 1/4 mile later pass Champion Farm on your right and continue ascending gently to the minor road beside Cumberhill Farm. Cross the road to the stile and footpath sign - Quarndon 2 miles. The path is faintly used as you keep the field edge on your right for almost two fields before passing through a gap and keeping the field boundary on your left to reach a stile beside a house before the minor road. Turn left along it towards Quarndon for almost 1/2 mile. Pass the cricket field on your right, and not long afterwards turn left along Coach Drive, signposted—Duffield via Bunker's Hill. At the end of the drive bear right through a stile and shortly afterwards gain a road. Turn right and at house No. 8 as signposted—Duffield, turn left on the path. In a few yards turn right, with the houses on your right and view on your left. The path is well stiled and leads you to Bunker's Hill. Just before it at the stile, the right of way keeps to the field edge and descends. But before following that it is worth continuing to the tree summit of Bunker's Hill to enjoy the extensive view.

Descend the path near the field edge on your left and pass Burley-wood Farm on your left after 1/4 mile. Just after turn left through the stile and follow the well-defined path to a gap in the next field and turn left on the path. Descend past a house to two stiles. Cross the farm drive to another stile and footbridge and ascend gently to a stile. Here bear right to the houses on the edge of Duffield and a stile. Cross the B5023 Wirksworth Road to the fenced path on your left between the houses. As you descend between the houses you cross several roads in the housing estate and the path is either to your right or left. You eventually reach the A6 road close to Kennings garage on your right. Cross over onto Makeney Road and just after the the next road fork turn right along Church Walk. This returns you to the footbridge over the railway and you can retrace your steps back to Duffield Church and nearby car park.

DUFFIELD—once had an impressive castle but was pulled down several centuries ago. The outline can still be seen on Castle Hill. The church dedicated to St. Alkmund is away from the main centre of the town and dates from the 12th century. The interior has several impressive monuments.

DERWENT VALLEY FROM BUNKERS HILL.

MACKWORTH CASTLE GATEHOUSE.

MARKEATON & MACKWORTH - 4 1/2 MILES

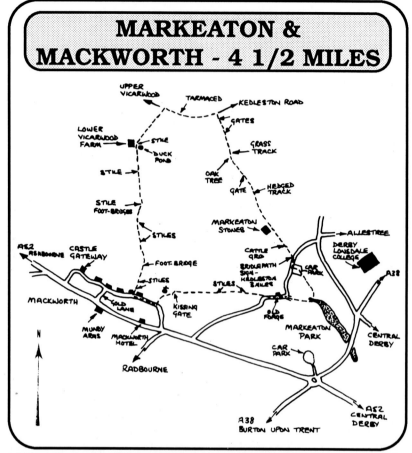

UPPER VICARWOOD

TARMACED

KEDLESTON ROAD

GATES

GRASS TRACK

LOWER VICARWOOD FARM

STILE

DUCK POND

STILE

OAK TREE

GATE

HEDGED TRACK

STILE FOOT-BRIDGE

MARKEATON STONES

A52 ASHBOURNE

CASTLE GATEWAY

STILES

CATTLE GRID

ALLESTREE

DERBY LONSDALE COLLEGE

FOOT-BRIDGE

BRIDLEPATH SIGN - KEDLESTON 3 MILES

CAR PARK

A38

MACKWORTH

GOLD LANE

STILES

STILES

OLD FORGE

KISSING GATE

CENTRAL DERBY

MUNDY ARMS

MACKWORTH HOTEL

MARKEATON PARK

N

RADBOURNE

CAR PARK

A52 CENTRAL DERBY

A38 BURTON UPON TRENT

MARKEATON PARK

32

MARKEATON AND MACKWORTH — 4 1/2 MILES
- allow 2 hours

•• •• ••• •• —Markeaton—Markeaton Stones—Lower Vicarwood Farm— Mackworth Brook—Mackworth—Mackworth Church—Markeaton Park— Markeaton.

—O. S. 1:25,000 Pathfinder Series Sheet No. SK 23/33—Derby and Etwall .

—Markeaton—just north of the village on the edge of Markeaton Park. A further one lies on the southern edge of the Park just off the A38 road.

ABOUT THE WALK—Markeaton Park is an enjoyable area and worth exploring to see the gardens, vegetable garden and lake, the haunt of Canada Geese. The walk explores the countryside to the west of the Park, providing views back to the city of Derby and the prominent Lonsdale College. Mackworth has a very attractive church situated in a field away from the village. Just off the route but worth seeing is the impressive gatehouse to the now disappeared Mackworth Castle. There is no inn actually on the route but The Mundy Arms in Mackworth is just 1/4 mile away!

WALKING INSTRUCTIONS—From the car park return to the road and turn right. A few yards later turn left on the tarmaced farm road, bridlepath signed— Kedleston. After 1/4 mile pass Markeaton Stones Farm on your left and continue on the hedged track to a gate 1/4 mile further on. Through this you enter a large field but the track guides you across to your right, passing a solitary oak tree to your left. Pass through a stile beside the next gate, and another gate shortly afterwards before a tarmaced farm road. Turn left and gently ascend, and a little over 1/4 mile later turn left onto another tarmaced track heading towards Lower Vicarwood Farm. At the entrance to the farm turn left to a stile with duck pond on your left. The next mile to Mackworth is very well stiled as you keep the field boundary (hedge) on your immediate left all the way until just before Mackworth. After 1/4 mile you cross the Mackworth Brook on a footbridge. As you near the village you walk up a hedged path.

Gaining the road in the village, to your right, a little over 1/4 mile away is the castle gateway. A few yards to your right is Gold Lane and at the top of this is the Mundy Arms. Turn left along the village road, and on the sharp righthand corner turn left onto the path to the church, dedicated to All Saints. Walk in front of the church and just beyond it diagonally to your left is the kissing gate and path to Markeaton. The path is well defined and stiled and in 1/2 mile reach the road on the village outskirts. Keep ahead passing the Old Forge on your left and Nurseries on your right. Where the road turns left—the car park is just up here—keep ahead and enter Markeaton Park. On reaching the lake turn left over the bridge and follow the path to your left to reach the car park.

MACKWORTH CASTLE—built by the Mackworth family in 1495 but only the impressive gateway remains.

LOWER VICAR FARM, NR. MACKWORTH.

REMEMBER AND OBSERVE THE COUNTRY CODE

 Enjoy the countryside and respect its life and work.

 Guard against all risk of fire.

Fasten all gates.

Keep your dogs under close control.

 Keep to public paths across farmland.

 Use gates and stiles to cross fences, hedges and walls.

  Leave livestock, crops and machinery alone.

 Take your litter home - pack it in; pack it out.

Help to keep all water clean.

 Protect wildlife, plants and trees.

 Take special care on country roads.

RADBOURNE - 4 1/2 MILES

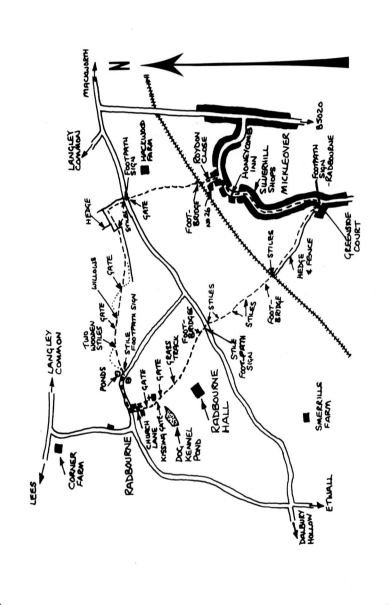

RADBOURNE—4 1/2 MILES
- allow 2 hours.

 —Slade Plantation—Radbourne Church—Radbourne—Silverhill Farm—Mickleover—Honeycomb Inn—Black Wood—Slade Plantation.

— 1:25,000 O.S. Pathfinder Series, Sheet No. SK 23/33 Derby and Etwall.

—No official one.

ABOUT THE WALK—Radbourne Hall is a stunning building and this walk takes you through the estate on reasonable paths, with glimpses of the building. You pass the church which contains several monuments and hatchments. You cross felds m the neighbourhood of Silverhill Farm, which in summer could be filled with crops making walking awkward and causing you to walk around the fields to get to the stiles. This section is short. You walk through the western edge of Silverhlll's housing estate in Mickleover, passing the only inn on the walk, the Honeycomb. The remainder of the walk is field and woodland walking on defined paths. I have started the walk on the minor road south of Radbourne Hall, but being circular you can start it anywhere.

WALKING INSTRUCTIONS—From the footpath sign and stile, beside the road, near Slade Plantation, head northwards on the defined path into woodland and soon cross a footbridge. Afterwards you soon reach a field and keep the woodland on your left. At the end of the woodland on your left you descend gently into a hollow bearing right slightly to gain a grass track. Shortly afterwards pass through a gate then right at the kissing gate to Radbourne Church. Keep to the left of it along the tarmaced path to the gate. Bear right along the lane—Church Lane —to the minor road. Turn right and follow the road round to your right for 1/4 mile to a small pond on your right and just ahead a path sign and stile on your left. As indicated by the sign the path diagonally ascends the field to your left, but as it is irregularly used there is no pathline to follow. If there are crops here, it is better to walk around the field boundary on your left to reach the wooden stiles. Continue across the next field well to the left of Silverhill Farm to a path gate. Through this cross the corner of the field to a pond site surrounded by willow trees, just ahead. You should now go diagonally across the field to a gate but a field boundary on your left has been removed. If the path line is not clear or full of crops it is better to walk along the field edge on your left for a short distance before turning right following the line of trees—on the right of them is the gate. Again the next field has been made into one large one and it is best to keep close to the field boundary on your right to reach the stile, little over 1/4 mile away. Here the difficult section ends. Keep the hedge on your left to the end of the field where turn right along the field edge to reach a stile and path sign beside the minor road.

Go straight across to the gate and keep the field edge on your right for the next three felds. The path soon gets defined as you approach the footbridge over the railway. Over this you enter the housing estate. Walk along Roydon Close to the main estate road. Turn right and keep on this road for the next 1/2 mile, passing the Honeycomb Inn on your right and shortly afterwards the shopping centre on your left. 1/4 mile later turn right into Greenside Court, also footpath signed — Radbourne. At the end of the houses turn left to the stile and follow the defined path along the field boundary on your left. In the third field you reach the stiles and cross the railway line. Ahead the path is well defined as you cross the stiled fields to the minor road beside Slade Plantation where you began.

RADBOURNE HALL—Built in 1750, it is a classical Georgian building of perfect proportions. The Chandos-Pole family have owned the Manor for several centuries. Bonnie Prince Charles had lunch here in 1745 before moving towards Derby.

THE HIKER'S CODE

❀ *Hike only along marked routes - do not leave the trail.*

❀ *Use stiles to climb fences; close gates.*

❀ *Camp only in designated campsites.*

❀ *Carry a light-weight stove.*

❀ *Leave the trail cleaner than you found it.*

❀ *Leave flowers and plants for others to enjoy.*

❀ *Keep dogs on a leash.*

❀ *Protect and do not disturb wildlife.*

❀ *Use the trail at your own risk.*

❀ *Leave only your thanks and footprints - take nothing but photographs.*

DALBURY AND TRUSLEY - 6 1/2 MILES

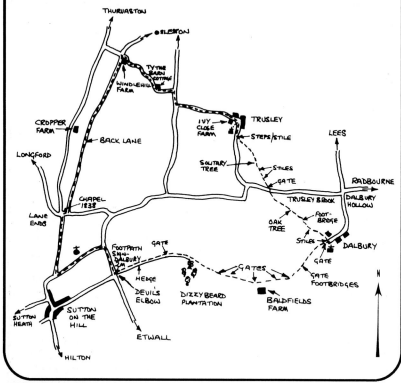

THURVASTON

OSLESTON

TYTHE BARN COTTAGE

WINDLEHILL FARM

CROPPER FARM

BACK LANE

IVY CLOSE FARM

TRUSLEY

STEPS/STILE

LEES

LONGFORD

SOLITARY TREE

STILES

GATE

RADBOURNE

CHAPEL 1838

TRUSLEY BROOK

DALBURY HOLLOW

LANE ENDS

OAK TREE

FOOT-BRIDGE

FOOTPATH SIGN-DALBURY 2M

GATE

STILES

DALBURY

HEDGE

GATES

GATE

DEVILS ELBOW

DIZZY BEARD PLANTATION

BALDFIELDS FARM

GATE FOOTBRIDGES

SUTTON HEATH

SUTTON ON THE HILL

ETWALL

HILTON

N

TRUSLEY CHURCH.

40

DALBURY AND TRUSLEY
—6 1/2 MILES - allow 3 hours.

   —Dalbury—Trusleybrook—Trusley—Windlehill
Farm—Four Lane Ends—Sutton on the Hill (church)—Devil's Elbow—
Baldfields Farm— Dalbury .

   —1:25,000 O.S. Pathfinder Series Sheet No SK 23/33—Derby
and Etwall.

—No official one.

ABOUT THE WALK—An area of Derbyshire walked rarely, which
is a shame for it IS full of history and peaceful countryside. Because
it is little walked the rights of way are sometimes hard to find or are
now lost! I hesitated for a while whether to include this walk as part
of it is along lanes as the rights of way are impassable. But on
reflection I felt it was wrong to discard it for the vicinity is worth
exploring and needs walking. I regret there is no inn on this walk—
sorry!

WALKING INSTRUCTIONS—Starting from Dalbury Church walk
to the end of the tarmaced road to the metal gate and turn right to
reach another gate. Through this bear left past the edge of a field to
a gap in the top lefthand corner of the next field. Bear slightly right
after this to reach a stile. Continue ahead bearing slightly left to reach
a footbridge over the stream. Across this bear right passing a solitary
oak tree to reach the left of the farm at Trusleybrook. There are no
stiles here or at the road just ahead. Cross the road to a gate and aim
for the lefthand corner of the field ahead where there is a stile. At the
end of the next field are two stiles. In the next field pass another tree
before hearing slightly left to reach some steps and a stile. Turn right
and walk through Trusley village passing the church on your left.

At the road junction 1/2 mile later turn right and soon afterwards left
along the winding lane past Tithe Barn Cottage to the road junction
at Windlehill Farm. Turn left along Back Lane for just over a mile.
Turn right then left and just over 1/4 mile later left to walk past the
solitary church of Sutton on the Hill. At the road junction shortly
after turn right, and at the next road junction, 1/4 mile later, leave
the road on your left, as footpath signed—Dalbury 2 miles. Go

through the gate and keep the hedge on your right to another gate after more than 1/4 mile. Continue beside the field edge to the end of Dizzybeard Plantation. Continue ahead across an open field until you walk beside the field edge on your right and gain another gate. Continue to another and still keep the field edge on your right to another gate close to Baldfields Farm. Keep to the left of it down the field to its lefthand corner and a gate. Through this turn left, with Dalbury church ahead, and reach a gate and footbridges. Over these keep the field edge on your left and reach a stile and your starting out route close to the church.

DALBURY CHURCH - dedicated to All Saints has the oldest piece of stained glass in Derbyshire— the figure of St Michael about 1200 A.D.

TRUSLEY CHURCH— has box pews and numerous hatchments of the Coke family, In the chancel in a glass case is a funeral garland, one of four used at the funeral of a Miss Webster. The making of garlands was a popular Midlands custom in the 18th century. Upon the death of an unmarried girl before her marraige, garlands were made and carried in the funeral procession. After the proceedings they were hung above the deceased person's pew. This is one of the few surviving examples .

DALBURY CHURCH.

CARVER'S ROCKS - FOREMARK WALK.

STAUNTON HAROLD CHURCH - MELBOURNE WALK.

43

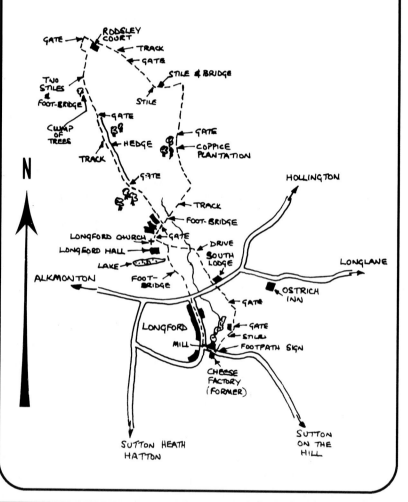

LONGFORD - 2 & 4 1/2 MILES

LONGFORD CHEESE FACTORY PLAQUE.

LONGFORD—2 & 4 1/2 MILES
- allow one and two hours.

 —Longford—Longford Church—Coppice Planta-tion—Rodsley Court—Longford Park—Longford Church—Longford.

 —1:25,000 O.S. Pathfinder Series Sheet No. SK 23/33—Derby and Etwall.

—No official one.

ABOUT THE WALK—Longford is a particularly attractive and interesting village with a magnificent mill and former cheese factory. The nearby hall and church are of more than passing interest and make a walk in this area extremely stimulating The shorter walk simply takes you through the village to the hall and church, while the longer one takes you into rural countryside to the north of the estate. There is no inn actually on the walk, but 1/2 mile away is the Ostrich Inn.

WALKING INSTRUCTIONS—Starting from the mill and former cheese factory walk along Longford Lane for a few yards to the path sign and fenced path beside the drive of Mill Close. Follow the path to a stile and cross the private driveway to the next stile and keep ahead with the fence on your left to a gate. Cross another driveway to a track and bear left along this to a gate on your right. You now enter a field which you cross to a small gate and footbridge in the far righthand corner. Over the bridge, followed by another gate, keep the hedge on your right to a stile before the Long Lane Road. Cross over as signposted—Public Bridleway and To the Church. Pass South Lodge and walk along the drive to Longford Church beside the hall. Here the two mile walkers return to the village as detailed later.

Those on the longer walk should go through the gate on the right of the farm buildings and walk on the right of the cow sheds to another gate. Through this gain a track and bridge over the stream. Just before it on your left is where you will be returning to after this circuit. Keep on the track for 1/4 mile, where it turns sharp left. Continue along it—now a hedged track—and in just over 1/4 mile gain a gate with Coppice Plantation on your left. Continue ahead on the track now in a large field. Follow it for the next 1/4 mile until you reach a gate on your right. Here turn left to a prominent stile and a clump of woodland. Over the stile cross a bridge to another and bear right up the field to a white painted gate. Here join a track and follow this to Rodsley Court. Walk past the farm and buildings to a white gate on your left. Turn right through this and keep to the edge of the field on your left to reach the two stiles and footbridge in the lefthand corner of the field. Over the stiles bear left and diagonally cross the field to the left of a clump of trees. In the top lefthand corner of the field is a small gate. Through this bear right and keep the hedge on your left as you now follow a track past woodland on your left and on to a gate with woodland on your right. Continue on the track past the Nursery wall on your right to the farm buildings of Longford Hall. Keep to the lefthand side of them to gain the gate you passed earlier. Turn left keeping to the lefthand edge of the buildings to regain the church. Here both routes join and follow the same route back into Longford village.

Turn left away from the church along the drive you walked along earlier and after a few yards turn right at the stile and walk past the wrought iron gates of the hall and on beside the pond stream to a footbridge. Cross this and follow the defined path to the road, reached via a stile beside a path sign. Cross over and walk along the road into Longford village, past the school and Post Office back to the mill.

LONGFORD — the Hall was built by the Longford family, and many monuments to them can be seen in the adjacent church. In the 17th century the Coke family lived in the Hall; another major Derbyshire family. In Longford village can be seen the impressive mill with wheel and water courses. Opposite is a large wooden building which, as detailed on its plaque, was the first cheese factory in England.

FORMER LONGFORD CHEESE FACTORY.

LONGFORD MILL.

DOVE BRIDGE - DOVERIDGE WALK.

CUBLEY - 5 MILES

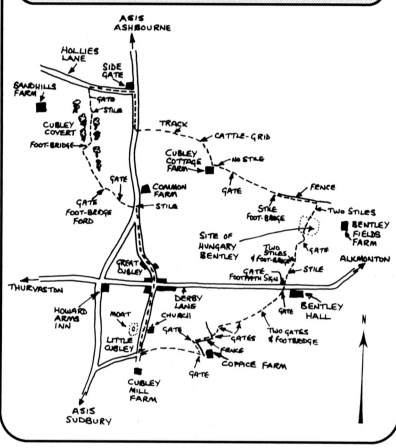

A5 IS
ASHBOURNE

HOLLIES
LANE

SIDE
GATE

SANDHILLS
FARM

GATE
STILE

CUBLEY
COVERT

FOOT-BRIDGE

TRACK

CATTLE-GRID

CUBLEY
COTTAGE
FARM

NO STILE

GATE

COMMON
FARM

FENCE

GATE

STILE

GATE

STILE
FOOT-BRIDGE

TWO STILES

FOOT-BRIDGE
FORD

SITE OF
HUNGARY
BENTLEY

TWO STILES
& FOOT-BRIDGE

GATE

BENTLEY
FIELDS
FARM

ALKMONTON

GREAT
CUBLEY

STILE

GATE
FOOTPATH SIGN

THURVASTON

HOWARD
ARMS
INN

MOAT

DERBY
LANE

CHURCH

GATE

GATES

TWO GATES
& FOOTBRIDGE

GATE

BENTLEY
HALL

LITTLE
CUBLEY

FENCE

COPACE FARM

GATE

CUBLEY
MILL
FARM

A5 IS
SUDBURY

N

**BENTLEY
HALL**

48

CUBLEY—5 MILES
- allow 2 1/2 hours

 —*Little Cubley—Coppice Farm—Bentley Hall— Site of Hungary Bentley—Cubley Cottage Farm—Cubley Covert— Great Cubley—Little Cubley.*

 —*1:25,000 O.S. Pathfinder Series Sheet No. SK 03/13—Uttoxeter.*

—*No official one.*

ABOUT THE WALK—Surprisingly, a forgotten walking area with the rights of way little used. I had to walk the area three times to discover usable rights of way, for some were just impenetrable or although path signed there was no access on the ground! Don't let that put you off, for the area is well worth walking in and I hope encourages people to explore the area. The walk starts from a remarkable church rich in history, from where you cross fields to the stunning Bentley Hall. After this you cross the site of the village of Hungary Bentley, which is fascinating. You return via fields and woodland before walking along the lane into Great and Little Cubley. No inn actually on the walk but the Howard Arms lies just over 1/4 mile off it on the A515 on the western edge of Great Cubley.

WALKING INSTRUCTIONS—Starting from the church in Little Cubley, continue southwards along the lane to the minor cross roads with Cubley Mill Farm just ahead. Turn sharp left up the tarmaced road and in little over 1/4 mile approach Coppice Farm. On its outskirts turn left through the gate into the field and keep the field edge on your right. At the next gate turn sharp right and keep the field edge on your right. At the next gate you bear diagonally left to a gate on your right 20 yards away. Here you cross a held passing an electric pole to reach another gate. In the next field continue ahead to another gate followed by footbridge and further gate. Ahead can be seen Bentley Hall as you cross the final held to a gate well to the left of it. Cross the Alkmonton/Great Cubley Road to the footpath sign and gate to your left. Keep to the edge of the field to a stile. Continue ahead on the lefthandside of the next field to two stiles and footbridge. Keep the field edge on your left as you walk round the field to a gate. This is not as the O.S. map shows but there is no stile in the corner. Continue into the next field keeping straight ahead and crossing the site of Hungary Bentley. Gain two stiles and cross a track, and at the field edge turn left and descend the field to a stile and brick bridge over Bentley Brook Ascend the field beyond to a gate in the top righthand corner. Keep the hedge on your left to the top of the field in front of Cubley Cottage Farm. There is no stile here. Over the fence gain the farm track and turn right along it to reach the AS 15 in less than 1/2 mile.

Turn right along the road to the first road on your left—Hollies Lane, beside Side Gate. Turn left along the lane and descend. At the bottom and before the small bridge, turn left through the gate gap and keep straight ahead to a small wooden gate. Just after pass stone gate pillars and enter a large field, keeping close to the fence on your right with woodland of Cubley Covert on the otherside. Ignore the first stile and 30 yards later ascend the second wooden stile. Walk past the pheasant enclosure and gain a break in the woodland and walk along this grassy swathe to the wood's edge by a small gate on your left. Turn right and cross a plank over the stream and reach a gate. Over this ascend the field for a few yards before turning left to a stile. Over this you aim for the righthand edge of the wood on your left where there is a gate, footbridge and ford. Cross and follow the track round to you right to a gate. Through this keep ahead for a short distance before bearing left to a wooden stile. On the other side cross the A515 road and descend the lane into Great Cubley. Cross the main road—Derby Road—and in just over 1/4 mile gain the church in Little Cubley.

GREAT CUBLEY - is the birthplace of Dr. Samuel Johnson's father.

LITTLE CUBLEY—has an exceptional church with many monuments to the Montgomery family. They lived here for 400 years and their home was opposite the church in a moated mansion, whose moat outline can still be seen today

LITTLE CUBLEY CHURCH.

DOVERIDGE & SOMERSAL HERBERT - 7 1/2 MILES

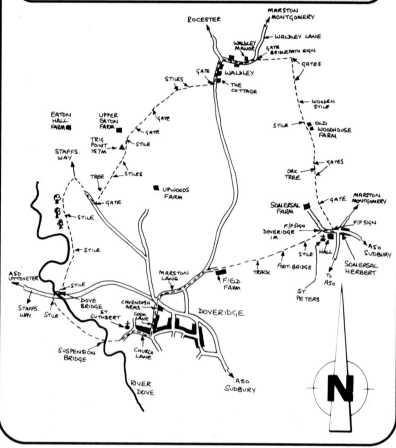

DOVERIDGE SUSPENSION BRIDGE

DOVERIDGE AND SOMERSAL HERBERT— 7 1/2 MILES
- allow 3 1/2 hours

 —Doveridge—River Dove—Dove Bridge—Staffordshire Way—Trig Point 157—Waldley—Somersal Herbert—Doveridge.

 —O.S. 1:25,000 Pathfinder Series Sheet No. SK 03 / 13—Uttoxeter.

—No official one.

ABOUT THE WALK—Starting from the church in Doveridge you cross a remarkable suspension bridge over the River Dove and on to the old Dove Bridge. Here you ascend above the river and cross the fields to the hamlet of Waldley. You now head due south to Somersal Herbert and its magnificent Elizabethan hall. A short field walk returns you to Doveridge where you can explore the church and historic yew tree. Much of the route is on little used rights of way, but all the stiles and gates are there. It is a delightful walk in unspoilt countryside away from the crowds and beside the south-western boundary of Derbyshire.

WALKING INSTRUCTIONS—Starting from Doveridge church dedicated to St Cuthbert, descend the road on the left of it to a layby on your left with parking space. Just to the right is the path which leads across to the river and suspension bridge. Cross the bridge and follow the raised path curving to your right to the A50 road and new bridge gained via a stile . Cross to another stile and gain Dove Bridge dated 1691 . Cross over to the stile on your left. Cross the field to the River Dove, and after a few yards beside it reach another stile. You now ascend following a faint path above the river and then on the right of woodland. After l/4 mile reach a stile and continue beside the trees on your left for another l/4 mile to the track from Eatonhall Farm and Staffordshire Way signs. Turn right along the track and cross a cattle grid close to a bridleway sign and onto a tarmaced road. A few yards later on your right is a wooden stile. Opposite on your left is a gate. Pass through this and ascend the field passing a solitary tree to a wooden stile. Continue ahead to another stile. Keep the field boundary on your left as it curves to your left and passes Trig Point 157, and gain a stile.

Over this turn right across the field to a gate and descend to another after crossing a small stream. As you descended you will have seen the houses of Waldley and these act as a guide as you aim for the righthand side of them. Cross the fields to the stiles and gates to reach the road opposite The Cottage. Turn left along the road past the houses and turn right onto the Marston Montgomery road. Just past Waldley Manor on your left go through the gate beside the bridlepath sign. Ascend for 1/4 mile to a gate and just afterwards another. Here turn right and head southwards to another gate. After this you descend to a stream and wooden stile. Ascend the field aiming for the righthand side of the farm ahead where there is a stile. Continue ahead down the farm track passing the farm on your left and round the end building as you descend to another stream, spanned by a bridge. Continue heading southwards for 1/2 mile to a gate and cross the next field passing a solitary oak tree to another gate. You now descend with Somersal Herbert ahead, which is entered via a stile beside the footpath sign—Marston Montgomery—and the Hall ahead.

Turn right past the church dedicated to St Peter and turn left onto the signposted path—Doveridge 1 mile. Cross the centre of the field to reach a footbridge over Marston Brook. 150 yards later reach the farm track which you follow past Field Farm to a minor road. Turn left along Marston Lane to the A50 road opposite the Cavendish Arms. Cross over and enter Doveridge along Cook Lane. After 1/4 mile turn right along Church Lane back to the church where you began.

DOVERIDGE—The church dedicated to St. Cuthbert dates from the century and has a very old yew tree. Here under its spreading branches Robin Hood and Maid Marion are reputed to have been married.

SOMERSAL HERBERT HALL—The finest Tudor building in Derbyshire and the village takes its name from the original owners, the Fitzherberts. The Fitzherberts still reside at Tissington Hall.

SOMERSAL HERBERT HALL.

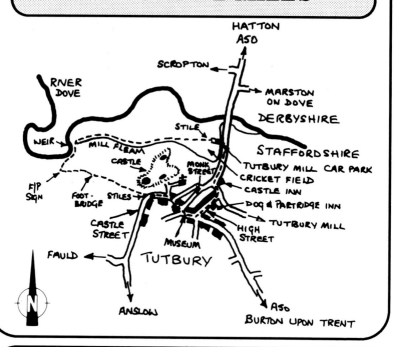

TUTBURY CASTLE—Dates from Norman times, but most of the ruins are of the 15th and 16th century when the castle was used as a "prison" for Mary, Queen of Scots. In the 17th century the castle was sieged during the Civil War and fell to the Parliamentarians. They ordered it to be destroyed but this was done spasmodically and accounts for todays scene.

TUTBURY—2 miles
- allow 1 hour; longer if visiting castle.

 —*Tutbury Mill car park—Mill Fleam—River Dove Weir—Tutbury— High Street—car park.*

 —*O.S. 1:25,000 Pathfinder Series Sheet No SK 22/32—Burton Upon Trent .*

 —*Tutbury Mill, off the A50 road on the northern fringe of the town.*

ABOUT THE WALK — Although Tutbury lies just over the border in Staffordshire I have included a short walk here as its history is so intertwined with Derbyshire and the tragic Mary, Queen of Scots. This walk encircles the impressive castle, and you are able to admire its setting from many angles. First you walk close to Tutbury's Mill Fleam to the River Dove and impressive weir. From here you head towards the righthandside of the castle to enter Tutbury. As you descend through the town you have options to explore the castle, church, and museum before passing the magnificent 15th century Dog and Partridge Inn.

WALKING INSTRUCTIONS—Head westwards out of the car park on the track to a stile and the cricket field on your left. Continue ahead, bearing slightly left to gain the path beside the Mill Fleam and follow it to the River Dove and weir. Turn left over the footbridge on the former sluice gates of the Fleam and walk along the river bank around the bend to your right for about 200 yards to the footpath sign. Don't go through the stile, but turn left with the hedge on your immediate right to the next stile and path sign. Here turn left and begin crossing the fields first to another pathsign and footbridge before gradually ascending to the righthand side of he castle. At the top ascend two stiles before gaining Castle Street. Turn left and descend the road with options of visiting the castle and church on your left. Continue past Monk Street, pass the Museum on your left and turn left into the High Street. Keep on this road back to the car park after passing the Dog and Partridge Inn. and shortly after the Castle Inn turn left back into the car park.

WILLINGTON AND TRENT & MERSEY CANAL - 2 1/2 MILES

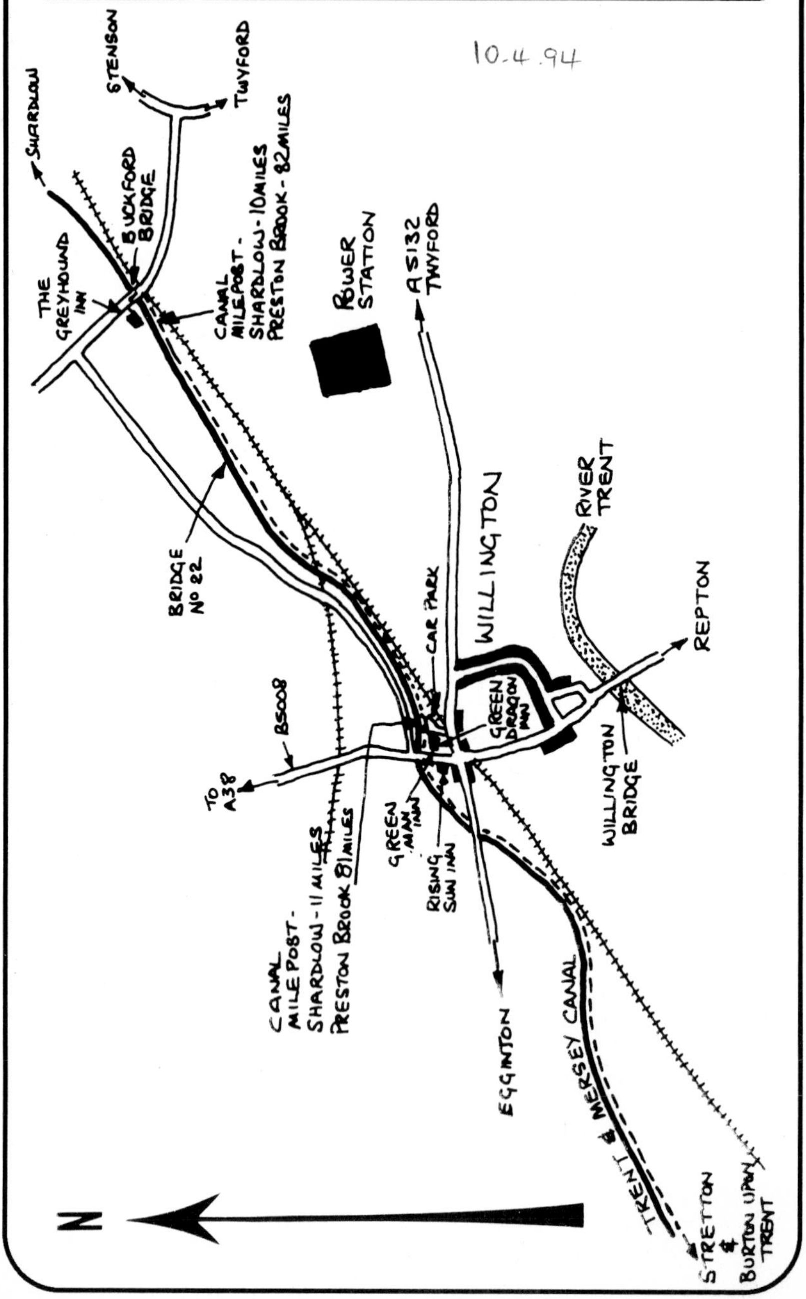

10.4.94

SHARDLOW

STENSON

TWYFORD

BUCKFORD BRIDGE

THE GREYHOUND INN

CANAL MILEPOST - SHARDLOW - 10 MILES PRESTON BROOK - 82 MILES

RIVER STATION

A5132 TWYFORD

BRIDGE NO 22

B5008

WILLINGTON

RIVER TRENT

REPTON

CAR PARK

GREEN DRAGON INN

WILLINGTON BRIDGE

TO A38

CANAL MILEPOST - SHARDLOW - 11 MILES PRESTON BROOK - 81 MILES

GREEN MAN INN

RISING SUN INN

EGGINTON

TRENT & MERSEY CANAL

STRETTON

BURTON UPON TRENT

N

58

WILLINGTON AND TRENT & MERSEY CANAL—2 1/2 MILES

- allow 1 hour.

 —*Willington—Trent & Mersey Canal—Buckford Bridge—and return same way*

 O.S. 1:25,000 Pathfinder Series, Sheet No. SK 22/32—Burton Upon Trent.

—*Willington Picnic Area.*

ABOUT THE WALK—With the River Trent to the south which effectively cuts off rights of way, there is little scope in the area for circular walks. However, the Trent & Mersey Canal provides delightful walking and this particular walk is to the pub and back! The towpath can be followed westwards to Stretton and the Derbyshire boundary and is again a very pleasant stroll. In both instances you return the same way.

WALKING INSTRUCTIONS—From the car park and picnic area gain the canal towpath and turn right. To your left is a canal milepost—Shardlow 11 miles / Preston Brook 81 miles . Turn right along the towpath and keep on it for just over a mile to the next milepost—Shardlow 10 miles / Preston Brook 82 miles . Just ahead is Buckford Bridge which you cross to reach The Greyhound Inn. Retrace your steps back to Willington.

GREYHOUND INN, NR. WILLINGTON.

59

BRETBY - 4 MILES

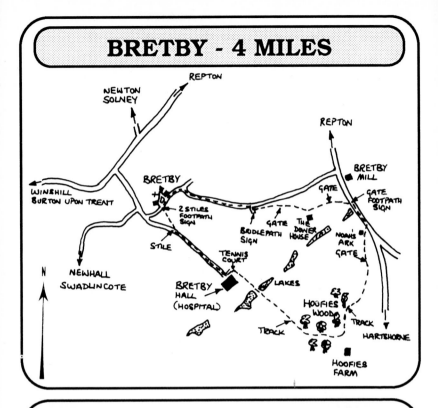

BRETBY HALL—a castle once stood here until being demolished and the stone used to build a large mansion. This too was demolished in the 18th century and the present Hall was built in 1813, by Sir Jeffrey Wyatville. He also designed the extension to Chatsworth House in the 19th century. The Hall is now a hospital.

BRETBY—4 MILES
- allow 1 3/4 hours

■● ■● ■● ■● —Bretby—Bretby Hall—Hoofies Wood—Noah's
Ark—The Dower House—Bretby.

🗺️ —1:25,000 O.S. Pathfinder Series Sheet No SK 22/32—Burton
Upon Trent.

🚗 —No official one.

ABOUT THE WALK—Bretby has a fascinating history and the
small hamlet is worth exploring while here. This short publess walk
takes you to the impressive Bretby Hall, now a hospital, and through
its grounds past lakes into woodland. You return along the northern
edge of the estate and a short extension enables you to see Bretby
Mill.

WALKING INSTRUCTIONS—Starting from the village triangle,
opposite is the stile and footpath sign—Bretby Hall. Leave the road
here and cross a footbridge and two stiles almost immediately before
following the defined path across the field to another stile and the
drive to Bretby Hall. Turn left along the drive and in 1/2 mile reach
the Hall. Turn left to the tennis courts and right almost immediately
onto the track which descends to inbetween the lakes. Continue
ahead on the track passing woodland on your immediate right before
open country, then into Hoofies Wood where you descend to its
eastern edge. Here is a cross roads of tracks. Take the upper left one
and keep on this for little over 1/2 mile as you walk through more of
Hoofies Wood then open felds, before woodland on your left near the
house—Noah's Ark. Here you descend the track to the minor road to
Repton.

Turn left and after 1/4 mile, just past a lake on your left, is the gate
and path sign. If you walk along the road a little further you can see
the impressive Bretby Mill building. Through the gate, bear right
ascending gradually to a metal gate. Turn left along the track and
keep to the righthand one after a few yards, ascend to where it levels
out opposite The Dower House. Here on your right is a gate. T urn
right and keep the field boundary on your right as you cross the
undulating ground to a small wooden gate in the far righthand corner
of the field. Here follow a good path through woodland to a road and
bridlepath sign. Turn right to the Bretby road and turn left and
ascend the road back into Bretby and its Green, where you began.

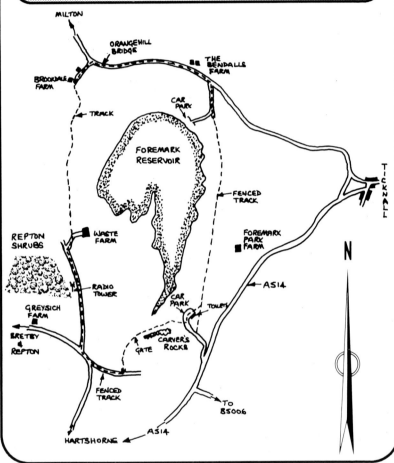

FOREMARK RESERVOIR - 6 MILES

MILTON

ORANGEHILL BRIDGE

THE BENDALLS FARM

BROOKDALE FARM

TRACK

CAR PARK

FOREMARK RESERVOIR

FENCED TRACK

TICKNALL

REPTON SHRUBS

WASTE FARM

FOREMARK PARK FARM

RADIO TOWER

A514

GREYSICH FARM

CAR PARK

TOILETS

BRETBY & REPTON

GATE

CARVER'S ROCKS

N

FENCED TRACK

TO B5006

HARTSHORNE

A514

FOREMARK RESERVOIR.

62

FOREMARK RESERVOIR
—6 MILES -allow 2 1/2 hours.

 —*Track on eastern side of reservoir—Bendalls Farm—Orangehill Bridge—Brookdale Farm—Waste Farm—Gravelpit Hill—Carver's Rocks— Car Park.*

—*1:25,000 O.S. Pathfinder Series Sheet No. SK 22/32—Burton Upon Trent.*

—*South Eastern end of Foremark Reservoir, near Carver's Rocks.*

ABOUT THE WALK—This walk encircles Foremark Reservoir, although for much of it you don't see it! Most of it is on good well defined tracks with distant views to the north over southern Derbyshire, with the Peakland hills on the horizon. The southern end is across fields and bracken to Carver's Rocks, where a short ascent returns you to the car park and its remarkable vantage point.

WALKING INSTRUCTIONS—Walk past the toilet block, at the northern end of the car park onto the path up to the fenced path (track). Turn left and keep on this track for the next 1 1/2 miles to the Ticknall road. After a mile you join the northern end car park road and descend this to the road. Turn left along road towards Milton, soon passing The Bendalls Farm on your right. Little over 1/2 mile later cross Orangehill Bridge. Shortly afterwards the road turns sharp right and you leave it by the second track on your left. This leads to Brookdale Farm, where the track swings left and ascends. Keep on this for the next mile gaining the farm drive of Waste Farm, on your left. Turn right along the drive and follow it round to your left past a radio mast on your right and the pine trees of Repton Shrubs. Keep on this to the Hartshorne Road. Turn left and a few yards later left onto a fenced track over Gravelpit Hill. Keep on this for 1/4 mile to a prominent hedged track on your left. Turn left along this wooded area to a field. The path is defined as you gently descend the field to a stile slightly on your right. Over this you enter the woodland and bracken of Carver's Rocks. In theory you keep straight ahead but in summer the bracken is tall almost forming a barrier. A little bit of weaving and pushing your way through along defined paths will bring you to the rocks. Here follow the well used path out of them back to the car park.

ANCHOR CHURCH & FOREMARK - 4 1/2 MILES

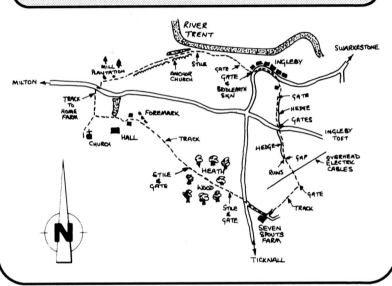

ANCHOR CHURCH.

ANCHOR CHURCH AND FOREMARK—4 1/2 MILES

—allow 2 hours

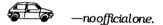 —*Ingleby—River Trent—Anchor Church—Mill Plantation— Foremark—Heath Wood—Seven Spouts Farm—Ingleby.*

—*O.S. 1:25,000 Pathfinder Series—Sheet No SK 22/32—Burton Upon Trent.*

—*no official one.*

ABOUT THE WALK—Starting from Ingleby you cross the fields to the River Trent before walking beside a rock escarpment containing the hermit's cave, known as Anchor Church. Leaving the river behind you ascend to the impressive Foremark Hall, now a school, and follow bridleways through woodland and fields back to Ingleby.

WALKING INSTRUCTIONS—In Ingleby follow the road round to your left (westwards) out of the village and follow the road as it turns sharp left, now heading southwards. On your right is Sycamore Farm and shortly afterwards the gate and bridlepath sign on your right. Go through the gate and ascend to the next gate. Continue on the path to another gate; here the bridlepath swings left, but the footpath right of way turns sharp right down the track before turning left along the top of the cliffs above the River Trent. The path is well defined as you descend to a stile at the base of the cliffs. After a few yards you leave the riverside and bear left along the path beneath the cliffs, beside a stretch of water. You soon reach Anchor Church on your left. Just after pass a spring and break in the cliffs. Keep ahead with the cliffs on your left to a young plantation—Mill Plantation. Here the right of way as marked on the ordnance survey map should go across the field; half left. But it does not exist on the ground; instead follow the track on the left of the plantation to the road, gained by a stile. Turn right then left onto Home Farm track.

Walk up the track for almost 1/4 mile to the first track on your left. Turn left along this passing the playing fields and lake on your left and Foremark Hall on your right. Follow the road round to your left past the classrooms to Foremark village and telephone kiosk. Where the road turns left keep ahead on the track and after 1/2 mile enter

Heath Wood via a stile. Continue on the track through the wood to another stile by a gate and continue on the track to the minor road. Cross over along the track to Seven Spouts Farm. At the farm turn left onto another track which keeps the wood on your immediate right. After 1/4 mile pass a small pond on your right and path. About 100 yards later leave the track via bridlepath gate on your left and ascend directly up the field, passing under the electric power lines to gain the righthand corner of the field where there is a field gap beside ruins of a building on its immediate left. Continue ahead, keeping the hedge on your left and reach a minor road via a gate. Cross over to the next gate and keep the hedge on your right to the next gate. In the next field still keep the hedge on your right to gain a gate and distinct path on your right in a wooded sunken depression. Descend this to a house on your left and descend the track drive to your left into Ingleby.

ANCHOR CHURCH—where a mediaeval hermit or 'anchorite' lived. The rocks have been carved out with windows, doors and pillars. Sadly the historic site has been abused.

FOREMARK HALL—the preparatory school for nearby Repton school. The hall was designed in Adam style by David Hiorns in 1762 for Sir Francis Burdett. The nearby church was built in the 1660's and is quite exceptional with wrought ironwork by Robert Bakewell and many memorials to the Burdett family.

TRENT & MERSEY CANAL, NEAR WILLINGTON.

DOG AND PARTRIDGE INN, TUTBURY.

MELBOURNE - 10 MILES

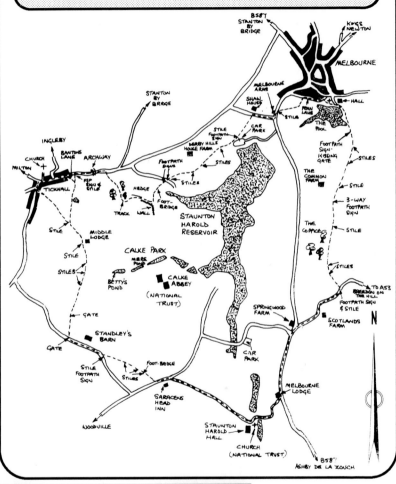

TICKNALL ARCHWAY.

MELBOURNE—10 MILES
- allow 4 to 5 hours.

'● '● '● '● —Melbourne—Staunton Harold Reservoir—Ticknall—Calke Park —Saracens Head (Heath End)—Staunton Harold Church—Melbourne Lodge —Scotland—The Pool, Melbourne.

 —1:25,000 O.S. Pathfinder Series, Sheet No. SK 22/32—Burton Upon Trent.

— 1 / Central Melbourne, near church.

2/ Staunton Harold Reservoir.

ABOUT THE WALK—The longest walk in the book but very much the grandslam of the premier historical buildings in Southern Derbyshire. From Melbourne you pass the church before gaining views over Staunton Harold Reservoir. Next you descend into Ticknall where a short diversion can be made to explore the church here. You then cross felds beside the woodland of Calke Park to Heath End. From here you descend to Staunton Harold and its remarkable Church and Hall before ascending to the A453 road. There are rights of way from here to Scotland but there is little evidence on the ground and it is easier to road walk round. From Scotland you pick up well defined paths leading back to Melbourne with its incomparable setting of Hall and lake making a fitting climax.

WALKING INSTRUCTIONS—Walk to Melbourne Church and turn right, walking past the lefthand side of it and gain Penn Lane. Turn left along the lane and after almost 1/4 mile, opposite Melbourne Clinic turn left onto the signposted footpath—Woodhouses. After a short distance bear right on the path and ascend gently, via the stiles to the B587 road. Turn left passing the Melbourne Inn on your right. Just after turn right, and after 1/4 mile opposite Shaw House turn left up the signed grass track. This soon brings you to near the old windmill with Staunton Harold Reservoir Car Park on the other side of the fence. Continue on the defined path to a stile and keep the field boundary on your immediate right for almost 1/2 mile, passing several stiles to reach a minor road via a stile and path sign.

Cross the road to the metal gate and path sign. This path is not defined but you descend the field to your right to a footbridge over the stream. The path is now defined as you ascend the field to a stone wall. Here turn right and keep the wall nearby on your left to the end of the field. Here you keep the hedge on your right as you descend slightly to a wood and track. Follow the track to your left around the wood and keep on it through woodland to reach the Ticknall road 1/4 mile later. Turn left into Ticknall passing under the archway. Just after on your left is the stile and path sign. If you are not going to explore Ticknall Church further up the road and on your right, turn here. If you are visiting the church you can take another path which is further round the corner on the B5006 road and joins the other path in little under 1/2 mile. Those not going to the church should turn left through the stile and keep to the field edge on your left to the next stile. For the next 1/2 mile keep the field edge on your right as you pass a small pond on your left. 1/4 mile later there is a stile on your left and defined path across the field. This is where the church party regains the main route. The pathline now leaves the field edge and crosses diagonally to your right to a stile well to the right of Middle Lodge. The path is defined as you keep close to the woodland on your left, with Calke Park on the other side. You pass through four stiles or gates and through woodland to reach the last field. Up to now the field boundary has been on your immediate left. You now cross the field to a small gate and reach the minor road near Standley's Barn. Turn left along the road for just over 1/4 mile to its sharp righthand bend. Here as footpath signed and stiled leave the road and keep the field edge on your left as you cross four fields, all stiled and a footbridge before the last one. Upon gaining the minor road turn left and soon pass the Saracens Head Inn and just after the entrance to Staunton Harold Hall and Church.

Turn right and walk along the drive to the church. Afterwards continue on the road past the lake on your right and ascend to Melbourne Lodge and the B587 road. In theory there is a right of way opposite to Scotland but it is extremely hard to follow. It is therefore better to turn left and walk along the road for 1/2 mile to Springwood Farm. Here turn right and pass Scotland Farm on your right, and 1/2 mile later just after a house on your left is a stile and footpath sign—a shoe shape. Turn left and follow the defined path down to a stile and stiles in the bottom. Here bear right keeping to the bottom of the dale, first with the field boundary on your immediate left. Just after passing a 3 way path sign the field boundary is on your right and the path is well defined as you approach Melbourne and its Pool. Keep ahead and walk round the righthand side of it to pass the Hall and regain the church where you began.

STAUNTON HAROLD CHAPEL—National Trust property and built by Sir Robert Shirley in 1653. The interior contains considerable Jacobean carvings including a magnificent screen and an English-built organ.

CALKE ABBEY—An Augustinian Priory was founded here in 1130. In 1621 Henry Harpur acquired the estate, and a later member of the family in the early 1700s began building the present quadrangular building, incorporating some of the monastic building. The adjacent parkland is home to a herd of deer. The estate is under the care of the National Trust and the house is well worth visiting to see where time has stood still.

MELBOURNE HALL—The Hall lies on the site of the residence of the Bishops of Carlisle who resided here for several centuries, as Melbourne Church was an endowment of the Bishopric of Carlisle. Much of the present building dates from the 18th century with the gardens a little earlier. The grounds are famed for its yew tunnel and wrought iron "birdcage" made by Robert Bakewell, the renowned ironsmith whose work can be seen in places in Derbyshire. Melbourne Church has considerable Norman workmanship and is well worth visiting to learn more of the Melbourne story and its association with Australia.

SHARDLOW - 3 MILES

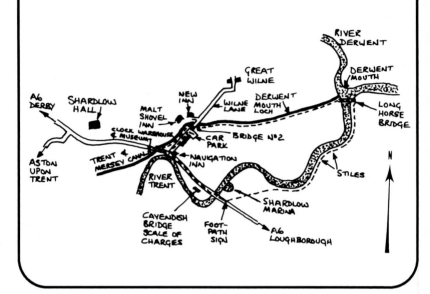

RIVER DERWENT

DERWENT MOUTH

GREAT WILNE

WILNE LANE

DERWENT MOUTH LOCK

LONG HORSE BRIDGE

A6 DERBY

SHARDLOW HALL

MALT SHOVEL INN

NEW INN

CLOCK WAREHOUSE & MUSEUM

CAR PARK

BRIDGE No 2

ASTON UPON TRENT

TRENT & MERSEY CANAL

NAVIGATION INN

STILES

N

RIVER TRENT

SHARDLOW MARINA

CAVENDISH BRIDGE SCALE OF CHARGES

FOOT-PATH SIGN

A6 LOUGHBOROUGH

CLOCK WAREHOUSE, SHARDLOW.

72

SHARDLOW—3 MILES
- Allow 1 1/2 hours.

 —*Shardlow—Trent & Mersey Canal—Derwent Mouth—Long Horse Bridge—River Trent—A6—Cavendish Bridge—Shardlow.*

 —*1:50,000—Sheet No. 129—Nottingham and Loughborough—1:25,000—Sheet No. SK 43/53—Nottingham (South West)*

—*Shardlow, off Wilne Lane.*

ABOUT THE WALK—Shardlow is one of the finest and best-preserved inland ports in England. This short walk follows the Trent & Mersey Canal through Shardlow to the junction of the River Trent and Derwent. You walk beside the Trent back to Shardlow, to explore fully the port and the Canal Museum in the Clock Warehouse.

WALKING INSTRUCTIONS—Turn right out of the car park along Wilne Lane to Bridge No. 2 over the canal. Turn left before the bridge and descend to the canal towpath; opposite is the Malt Shovel and New Inn. Turn right and follow the towpath for almost a mile to the rivers Trent and Derwent. After 3/4 mile pass the Derwent Mouth Lock. Cross the footbridge over the River Trent (Long Horse Bridge) and turn right. Walk along the banks of the River Trent for almost 3/4 mile to where the river turns sharp left. Here continue straight ahead across the field to a stile and footpath sign on the immediate left of a large building complex on your right.

Over the stile gain the A6 road and turn right over the Cavendish Bridge with Shardlow Marina on your right. Continue on into Shardlow, passing the plaque on your left of the scale of charges used on the bridge. Pass the entrance to Wilne Lane and the Navigation Inn to reach the canal. The towpath as signed is on your right, but before following it continue along the A6 to visit the Clock Warehouse on your left. Retrace your steps back to the towpath and walk along it to Bridge No. 2 and ascend back to Wilne Lane. Turn right back to the car park.

SHARDLOW—Major canal location with the start of the 92 mile Trent & Mersey Canal. The village is worth exploring to see this classic inland port and numerous buildings associated with the canal era.

ELVASTON CASTLE & THULSTON - 3 MILES

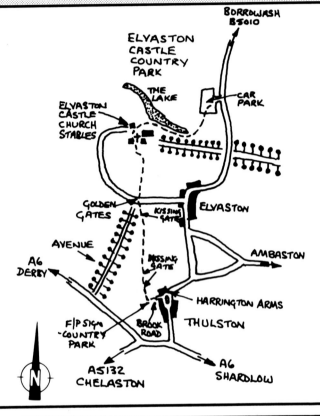

ELVASTON CASTLE COUNTRY PARK

THE LAKE

BORROWASH B5010

CAR PARK

ELVASTON CASTLE CHURCH STABLES

GOLDEN GATES

KISSING GATE

ELVASTON

AVENUE

AMBASTON

A6 DERBY

MISSING GATE

HARRINGTON ARMS

F/P SIGN -COUNTRY PARK

BROOK ROAD

THULSTON

N

A5132 CHELASTON

A6 SHARDLOW

GOLDEN GATES, ELVASTON CASTLE.

ELVASTON CASTLE AND THULSTON—3 MILES
- allow 2 hours

  —*Car Park—The Lake—Elvaston Castle and church—gardens— Golden Gates—Thulston—return the same way.*

—*O.S. 1:25,00 Pathfinder series—Sheet No SK 43 / 53—Nottingham (South West).*

—*Elvaston Castle, just off the B5010 road.*

ABOUT THE WALK—Elvaston Castle and its grounds is an enthralling and historical Country Park and extremely well worth exploring. A very pleasant day can be spent visiting the park's main features. The walk is a short one so that you can see much of the area while crossing the park to Thulston and the Harrington Arms Inn. You retrace your steps back to the car park.

WALKING INSTRUCTIONS—From the car park follow the paths to the lake and onto the castle and church. Walk through the famous topiary gardens to the south of the church and castle and reach the Golden Gates—painted blue! Just ahead to your left is a kissing gate. Pass through this and follow the defined path across the field to another kissing gate. Shortly after this one reach a metal kissing gate and follow the path round to your left to Brook Road and path sign—Country Park. To your left is the Harrington Arms Inn. Return the same way.

ELVASTON CASTLE—Built by the Stanhope family who in 1817 completely rebuilt it in Gothic style. The Stanhopes became the Earls of Harrington and the third Earl is responsible for making tea drinking todays national drink! The church contains monuments to the Harringtons. The beauty of the estate are its avenue of trees, topiary, and the Golden Gates, that came from a royal palace in Madrid. In 1969 the estate was purchased by the Derby Corporation and Derbyshire County Council who have made it into a country park.

EQUIPMENT NOTES

- Some personal thoughts

BOOTS - preferably with a full leather upper, of medium weight, with a vibram sole. I always add a foam cushioned insole to help cushion the base of my feet.

SOCKS - I generally wear two thick pairs as this helps minimise blisters. The inner pair are of loop stitch variety and approximately 80% wool. The outer are a thick rib pair of approximately 80% wool.

WATERPROOFS - for general walking I wear a T shirt or cotton shirt with a cotton wind jacket on top. You generate heat as you walk and I prefer to layer my clothes to avoid getting too hot. Depending on the season will dictate how many layers you wear. In soft rain I just use my wind jacket for I know it quickly dries out. In heavy or consistant rain I slip on a neoprene lined gagoule, and although hot and clammy it does keep me reasonably dry. Only in extreme conditions will I don overtrousers, much preferring to get wet and feel comfortable. I never wear gaiters!

FOOD - as I walk I carry bars of chocolate, for they provide instant energy and are light to carry. In winter a flask of hot coffee is welcome. I never carry water and find no hardship from not doing so, but this is a personal matter! From experience I find the more I drink the more I want and sweat. You should always carry some extra food such as Kendal Mint Cake, for emergencies.

RUCKSACKS - for day walking I use a climbing rucksack of about 40 litre capacity and although it leaves excess space it does mean that the sac is well padded, with an internal frame and padded shoulder straps. Inside apart from the basics for one day I carry gloves, balaclava, spare pullover and a pair of socks.

MAP & COMPASS - when I am walking I always have the relevant map - preferably 1:25,000 scale - open in my hand. This enables me to constantly check that I am walking the right way. In case of bad weather I carry a compass, which once mastered gives you complete confidence in thick cloud or mist.

WALK RECORD CHART.

DATE WALKED

DALE AND LOCKO PARK—4 1/2 MILES ....

MORLEY AND HORSLEY CARR- 4 1/2 MILES ....

BELPER AND CHEVIN—6 MILES ....

IDRIDGEHAY AND IRETON WOOD—5 MILES ....

MUGGINGTON AND WESTON UNDERWOOD
—4 M.ILES..

DUFFIELD AND BUNKER'S HILL—6 MILES ....

MARKEATON AND MACKWORTH—4 1/2 MILES ....

RADBOURNE—4 1/2 MILES ....

DALBURY AND TRUSLEY—6 l/2 MILES ....

LONGFORD—2 AND 4 1/2 MILES ....

CUBLEY—5 MILES ....

DOVERIDGE AND SOMERSAL HERBERT
—7 1/2 MILES ....

TUTBURY—2 MILES ....

WILLINGTON AND TRENT & MERSEY CANAL
2 1/ 2MILES..

BRETBY—4 MILES ....

FOREMARK RESERVOIR—6 MILES ....

ANCHOR CHURCH AND FOREMARK
—4 1/2 MILES ....

MELBOURNE—10 MILES..

SHARDLOW—3 MILES ....

ELVASTON CASTLE AND THULSTON
—3 MILES ....

THE JOHN MERRILL WALK BADGE

Complete six of the walks in this book and get the above special walk badge. Badges are a black cloth with walking man embroidered in four colours and measure - 3 1/2" in diameter.

BADGE ORDER FORM

Date and details of walks completed ....

....

NAME ....

ADDRESS ....

....
Price: £2.00 each including postage, VAT and signed completion certificate. Amount enclosed (Payable to JNM Publications) ....
From: JNM PUBLICATIONS, Winster, Matlock,
Derbyshire. DE4 2DQ.

℡ Winster (062988) 454 - 24hr answering service.
FAX: Winster (062988) 416

************* YOU MAY PHOTOCOPY THIS FORM *************

"I'VE DONE A JOHN MERRILL WALK" T SHIRT - Emerald Green with white lettering and walking man logo. Send £5.50 to JNM Publications stating size required.

OTHER BOOKS by JOHN N. MERRILL PUBLISHED by JNM PUBLICATIONS

CIRCULAR WALK GUIDES -
SHORT CIRCULAR WALKS IN THE PEAK DISTRICT
LONG CIRCULAR WALKS IN THE PEAK DISTRICT
CIRCULAR WALKS IN WESTERN PEAKLAND
SHORT CIRCULAR WALKS IN THE STAFFORDSHIRE MOORLANDS
SHORT CIRCULAR WALKS AROUND THE TOWNS & VILLAGES OF
THE PEAK DISTRICT
SHORT CIRCULAR WALKS AROUND MATLOCK
SHORT CIRCULAR WALKS IN THE DUKERIES
SHORT CIRCULAR WALKS IN SOUTH YORKSHIRE
SHORT CIRCULAR WALKS IN SOUTH DERBYSHIRE
SHORT CIRCULAR WALKS AROUND BUXTON
SHORT CIRCULAR WALKS IN THE HOPE VALLEY
40 SHORT CIRCULAR WALKS IN THE PEAK DISTRICT
CIRCULAR WALKS ON KINDER & BLEAKLOW
SHORT CIRCULAR WALKS IN SOUTH NOTTINGHAMSHIRE
SHIRT CIRCULAR WALKS IN CHESHIRE

CANAL WALKS -
VOL 1 - DERBYSHIRE & NOTTINGHAMSHIRE
VOL 2 - CHESHIRE & STAFFORDSHIRE
VOL 3 - STAFFORDSHIRE
VOL 4 - THE CHESHIRE RING
VOL 5 - LINCOLNSHIRE & NOTTINGHAMSHIRE
VOL 6 - SOUTH YORKSHIRE
VOL 7 - THE TRENT & MERSEY CANAL

JOHN MERRILL DAY CHALLENGE WALKS -
WHITE PEAK CHALLENGE WALK
DARK PEAK CHALLENGE WALK
PEAK DISTRICT END TO END WALKS
STAFFORDSHIRE MOORLANDS CHALLENGE WALK
THE LITTLE JOHN CHALLENGE WALK
YORKSHIRE DALES CHALLENGE WALK
NORTH YORKSHIRE MOORS CHALLENGE WALK
LAKELAND CHALLENGE WALK

INSTRUCTION & RECORD -
HIKE TO BE FIT.....STROLLING WITH JOHN
THE JOHN MERRILL WALK RECORD BOOK

MULTIPLE DAY WALKS -
THE RIVERS'S WAY
PEAK DISTRICT: HIGH LEVEL ROUTE
PEAK DISTRICT MARATHONS
THE LIMEY WAY
THE PEAKLAND WAY

COAST WALKS & NATIONAL TRAILS -
ISLE OF WIGHT COAST PATH
PEMBROKESHIRE COAST PATH
THE CLEVELAND WAY

PEAK DISTRICT HISTORICAL GUIDES -
DERBYSHIRE INNS - an A to Z guide
HALLS AND CASTLES OF THE PEAK DISTRICT & DERBYSHIRE
TOURING THE PEAK DISTRICT & DERBYSHIRE BY CAR
DERBYSHIRE FOLKLORE
PUNISHMENT IN DERBYSHIRE
CUSTOMS OF THE PEAK DISTRICT & DERBYSHIRE
WINSTER - a souvenir guide
ARKWRIGHT OF CROMFORD
TALES FROM THE MINES by Geoffrey Carr
PEAK DISTRICT PLACE NAMES by Martin Spray

JOHN MERRILL'S MAJOR WALKS -
TURN RIGHT AT LAND'S END
WITH MUSTARD ON MY BACK
TURN RIGHT AT DEATH VALLEY
EMERALD COAST WALK

COLOUR GUIDES -
THE PEAK DISTRICT.........Something to remember her by.

SKETCH BOOKS -
NORTH STAFFORDSHIRE SKETCHBOOK by John Creber

IN PREPARATION -
LONG CIRCULAR WALKS IN STAFFORDSHIRE
SHORT CIRCULAR WALKS IN WEST YORKSHIRE
SHORT CIRCULAR WALKS IN THE YORKSHIRE DALES
SHORT CIRCULAR WALKS IN THE LAKE DISTRICT
SHORT CIRCULAR WALKS IN NORTH YORKSHIRE MOORS
RUTLAND WATER CHALLENGE WALK
SNOWDONIA CHALLENGE WALK
FOOTPATHS OF THE WORLD - Vol 1 - NORTH AMERICA
HIKING IN NEW MEXICO

☞ Full list from JNM PUBLICATIONS, Winster, Matlock, Derbys.